Green Sr
Recipes

The Healthiest And Tastiest Green Smoothies For Lasting Weight Loss And Energy

By Jessica Brooks

Second Edition

The trademarks that are used are without any consent, and the publication of the trademark is without permission or backing by the trademark owner. All trademarks and brands within this book are for clarifying purposes only and are the owned by the owners themselves, not affiliated with this document.

Disclaimer – Please read!

The information provided in this book is designed to provide helpful information on the subjects discussed. This book is not meant to be used, nor should it be used, to diagnose or treat any medical condition. For diagnosis or treatment of any medical problem, consult your own physician. The publisher and author are not responsible for any specific health or allergy needs that may require medical supervision and are not liable for any damages or negative consequences from any treatment, action, application or preparation, to any person reading or following the information in this book. References are provided for informational purposes only and do not constitute endorsement of any websites or other sources. Readers should be aware that the websites listed in this book may change.

Table of Contents

Introduction

The goal of this book is to show you how to easily prepare green smoothies for every part of your dieting schedule. You'll learn about some appropriate smoothies that you can use during your cleansing period or find out which smoothies provide enough energy after a heavy workout.

If on the other hand you just want to make some delicious green smoothies, then you'll find recipes that are suitable for every time of the day.

Before going through the recipes on your own, check out the first chapter of this book and see what are some of the biggest health and life benefits of the usage of green smoothies and why they're better than regular vegetable or fruit shakes.

Hope you find this book valuable and that this list of 100 green smoothies helps you go through your diet regime.

Jessica Brooks

Health & Life Benefits of Green Smoothies

You've probably seen some of your co-workers drinking a mysterious green liquid during lunchtime. It was probably strange for you that they don't need anything else like a hamburger or french fries afterwards.

Well, that's the power of green smoothies. They provide enough energy for your body and enough nutrients for the whole day while avoiding unhealthy products full of sodium or artificial sweeteners yet managing to be extremely delicious.

You can be very creative when making your green smoothie and the products that you'll notice that are a part of almost every recipe are kale, spinach, asparagus, broccoli, brussels sprouts and every other green vegetable.

This doesn't meant that you must focus on green vegetables only as a part of your smoothie. Stuff like nuts; fruits including mango, papaya, pineapple and coconut; almond milk, soy milk, coconut water, variety of spices and many other things can be a part of your green smoothie recipe.

The increased levels of energy is probably one of the main reasons why you should try using green smoothies. You get lots of energy from these drinks because they can have enough proteins, carbs and fats in them, but your metabolism is able to digest them faster than solid foods, leaving all of the energy to be used by other parts of your body.

Why you should avoid using only fruits in your smoothie? Although they're a great source of vitamins and minerals, only green vegetables can offer a sufficient amount of fiber, which is a crucial part of your nutrition because of the role fibers play in the creation of energy for the body.

Another aspect to consider is the fact that green smoothies are easy to prepare and you can make huge amounts of them and use them for couple of days.

So, just to conclude, green smoothies are good because they:
- Offer pure nutrition;
- Healthier than fruit or vegetable juices;
- Easy and quick to make;
- Inexpensive;
- Lasting source of energy;
- Easy to digest.

Top Ten Post Workout Green Smoothies

Zucchini & Almond Iron Bomb

Ingredients:
- 2 cups chopped zucchini,
- 1 tablespoon cacao powder,
- 1 tablespoon sunflower seed butter,
- 1 cup almond milk,
- 3 tablespoons lemon juice
- 1 cup ice,
- dash of cinnamon

Instructions:
Peel the zucchini before you chop it and blend it together with the sunflower seed butter and cacao powder for about two minutes before adding the almond milk and ice. The cinnamon is optional and you can replaced it with rinsed dark chocolate or little bit of dried almonds on the top.

Jessica Brooks

Shiro Plum & Kale Energizer

Ingredients:
- 2 cups kale,
- 2 shiro plums,
- 1/2 cup fresh raspberries or strawberries,
- 1/4 cup oats,
- 1 teaspoon flax seed,
- ¼ cup raisins,
- ¼ cup nuts,
- ½ cup water,
- 1 cup ice.

Instructions:
Blend the kale together with the plums, oats, raisins, nuts and water for around 2 minutes before adding the raspberries. After half a minute of mixing just add the rest of the ingredients and blend until smooth.

Maple Water & Kale

Ingredients:
- 3 cups baby kale,
- ½ banana,
- ¼ cup strawberries,
- ¼ cup nuts,
- ¼ cup oats,
- 1 tablespoon coconut oil,
- ½ cup maple water,
- 1 cup ice cubes.

Instructions:
Blend the greens together with the banana and strawberries for about a minute before adding the strawberries, nuts and oats. After minute of blending add the coconut oil, maple water and ice and continue for another 2 minutes or until everything is smooth.

Cinnamon & Peanut Butter Muscle Builder

Ingredients:

- 3 cups collard greens,
- 1 banana,
- ½ red apple,
- 1 teaspoon cinnamon,
- 1 tablespoon peanut butter,
- ¼ cup oats,
- ½ cup water,
- ½ cup almond milk
- 1 cup ice.

Instructions:

Mix the vegetables and fruits together at first and blend for about 30 seconds before adding the peanut butter, cinnamon and almond milk. After a minute add the oats together with water and ice and blend until smooth.

Persian Greener

Ingredients:
- 3 cups kale,
- 1 Persian cucumber,
- ½ mango or papaya,
- 2 tablespoon hummus,
- 1 tablespoon lime juice
- ½ cup soy milk,
- ½ cup water,
- 1 cup ice.

Instructions:
Chop the Persian cucumber and blend it together with the kale and the mango/papaya half. Add the hummus and cacao powder together with the soy milk. Blend for about two minutes before adding the ice and water.

The BCS Post Workout King

Ingredients:

- 1 cup spinach,
- 1 banana,
- 1/2 cup coconut milk,
- 1 teaspoon walnut oil,
- 1 teaspoon flax seed,
- 1 tablespoon dry coconut,
- 1 cup of ice.

Instructions:

It's probably best to blend the banana and spinach first before adding the coconut milk together with the rest of the ingredients. You can add ½ a cup of fresh pineapple in the mix as it's always a good combination with banana and coconut.

The Sweet Potato, Mint & Coffee Awakener

Ingredients:

- ½ cup sweet potato, frozen,
- 2 cups almond milk,
- ½ cup mint,
- 1 teaspoon maple syrup,
- 1 teaspoon instant coffee (preferably Nescafe),
- 1 tablespoon ground chia seeds.

Instructions:

If you plan your meals the day before, you should cook the sweet potato and leave it in the freezer overnight. The other option is to add one cup of freshly cooked sweet potato together with 1 cup of ice. Blend the sweet potato together with the almond milk and maple syrup first. Pour ⅛ cup of boiling water over the instant coffee in a separate bowl and let it cool. Put it together with the chia seeds and fresh mint into the main mix and blend a little bit more. You can put a dash of dried coconut or cinnamon on top for taste.

Pistachio & Spinach Relaxation

Ingredients

- 4 tablespoons pistachios,
- 1 tablespoon hemp seeds,
- 1/2 cup fresh spinach,
- 1/2 cup almond milk,
- 1 cup Ice.

Instructions:

Make sure that the pistachios are peeled before you put them in the blender as their shell is pretty hard. Also try to use unsweetened almond milk or even better make one on your own using fresh almonds. Blend the pistachios, spinach and almond milk together at first as you would like to get most of that taste in the smoothie. Great smoothie for muscle rejuvenation.

Apple Crisp Smoothie

Ingredients:
- 3 cups baby romaine,
- 1 apple,
- ¼ cup oats,
- ¼ cup nuts,
- 1 teaspoon coconut oil,
- 1 cup water,
- 1 cup ice.

Instructions:
Chop the apple and blend it together with the baby romaine, water and coconut oil. After half a minute of blending add the oats, nuts and ice and continue for about two minutes.

Kalmond Routine

Ingredients:
3 cups kale,
1 banana,
2 tablespoons dehydrated coconut,
1 tablespoon cacao powder,
2 tablespoons almonds,
1 cup almond milk,
1/2 cup ice cubes.

Instructions:
Start with the banana and kale before adding the almonds and almond milk. Blend these ingredients until you get a nice mixture and then add the dehydrated coconut and cacao powder together with the ice cubes. Add everything in blender starting with greens and blend on high for two minutes. Then add ice and blend again until smooth.

Top Twenty High Fiber Green Smoothies

SAC Smoothie (Spinach, Asparagus and Cantaloupe)

Ingredients:

- 4 asparagus spears,
- 1 cup fresh spinach,
- 1 cup cantaloupe dices,
- 1 green apple,
- 1/2 cup unsweetened almond milk,
- 1 teaspoon flax oil,
- 1 cup ice.

Instructions:

Trip the asparagus spears and cut up the cantaloupe on tiny dices for a better blend. You should do the same with the apple before you add the almond milk. The flax oil is optional, but you should know that it makes the smoothie even better when we talk about absorption of the fiber.

The Broccoli Fiber Bomb

Ingredients:

- 2 cups broccoli,
- 1 cup almond milk,
- 1 cup blueberries or strawberries,
- 1 kiwi,
- 2 tablespoons chia seeds,
- 1 cup ice,
- ½ cup dried fruits.

Instructions:

Place the ice, boiled broccoli, chia seeds and dried fruits in the blender and try to get a firm mixture before adding the almond milk together with the blueberries and the kiwi. You should get a tasty yet fiber rich smoothie.

Carromato Celerius

Ingredients:

- 2 medium sized carrots,
- 2 medium sized tomatoes,
- 1 stalk of celery,
- 1 teaspoon black pepper,
- ½ cup ice,
- 1 tablespoon lemon juice,
- 1 tablespoon macadamia nut oil,
- Dash of pink salt,
- Dash of basil.

Instructions:

Believe it or not even a smoothie made out of tomatoes and carrots can be tasty and rich with useful nutrients. Mix the carrots, celery, tomatoes and hemp seed with the ice first and then add everything else. The salt and basil are optional.

Mint Bubble Gum

Ingredients:

- 1 cup hemp milk,
- 1 cup coconut water,
- 1 tablespoon flax seed,
- 1 tablespoon chia seed,
- 1 cup baby spinach,
- 1 tablespoon cacao nibs,
- ½ medium sized avocado,
- 3 teaspoons dried mint,
- 1 cup ice.

Instructions:

Mixing avocado with mint will make this smoothie taste like those "hubba bubba" bubble gums from your childhood. Blend the ice with the mint and avocado. After that first add the hemp milk and coconut water before mixing everything together.

Beet Sprouts Juice

Ingredients:

- 1 cup water,
- 1 medium avocado, diced,
- 1 cup celery stalks, chopped,
- 1 medium beet, boiled & chopped,
- ½ cup brussels sprouts,
- 3 tablespoons lime juice,
- 2 tablespoons flax seed,
- 4 large ice cubes.

Instructions:

Boil the beet until it gets soft. It's better to peel the beet after it has cooked, but make sure to use gloves or plastic bags because you may end up with red stains on your hands. Add the beet and the avocado in the blender together with the cup of water. After you get a firm mixture add everything else in the blender.

Cabbage Delight

Ingredients:

- 1 cup orange juice,
- ½ cup fresh blueberries,
- 1 ½ cup cabbage, chopped,
- ¼ cup fresh almonds,
- 1 cup ice cubes,
- ½ cup soy milk.

Instructions:

Who said that cabbage can't be delicious? Just put all of these ingredients in the blender and mix them for a minute, this smoothie is best served fresh out of the blender.

Tahini & Baby Kale Combo

Ingredients:
- 3 cups baby kale,
- 1 banana,
- 1/2 cup raspberries,
- 1 tablespoon tahini,
- 1 teaspoon flax oil,
- 1 tablespoon chia seed,
- 1 cup water,
- 1/2 cup ice cubes.

Instructions:
Add everything in blender starting with greens and blend on high for two minutes. Then add ice and blend again until smooth

Bitter Melon For The Experienced

Ingredients:
- 2 cups baby kale,
- 1 pear,
- ¼ cup bitter melon,
- ¼ cup oats,
- ½ cup almonds,
- 1 cup water,
- 1 cup ice.

Instructions:
Chop the bitter melon and get rid of the seeds from the inside. Add everything in blender starting with greens and blend on high for two minutes. Then add ice and blend again until smooth.

Mango Go Go Go!!!

Ingredients:
- 2 cups spinach,
- 1 cup frozen mango,
- ½ cup baby carrots,
- ½ cup coconut water,
- ¼ cup orange juice,
- 2 tangerines, peeled,
- ½ cup yogurt.

Instructions:
Start with the spinach, baby carrots, coconut water, tangerines and orange juice before adding the frozen mango and yogurt. Don't need the ice because your mango is already frozen.

Tropical Green Smoothie

Ingredients:

- 1 ½ cups fresh spinach,
- 1 cup unsweetened coconut water,
- 1 cup pineapple, frozen,
- ¼ avocado.

Instructions:

- Place all of the ingredients into a blender and blend until completely smooth.
- Serve immediately.

Oatilicious

Ingredients:
- 2 cups spinach,
- 1 cup frozen peaches,
- ½ cup fresh banana,
- ½ cup raw zucchini,
- ¾ cup coconut water,
- ½ cup plain yogurt,
- 3 tablespoons cacao powder,
- 2 Tablespoon wheat germ.

Instructions:
Blend the banana, spinach, zucchini and coconut water first, before adding the frozen peaches together with the yogurt and wheat germ.

Cherry Berry Ginger Smoothie

Ingredients:
- 1 cup frozen cherries,
- 1 cup strawberries,
- 1 cup kale
- 1/8 cup walnuts,
- 1 teaspoon wheat germ,
- ½ teaspoon freshly grated ginger,
- ¾ cup of cold green tea.

Instructions:
- Place all of the ingredients into a blender and blend until completely smooth.
- Serve immediately.

The Mango-Rita

Ingredients:
- 2 cups of fresh spinach,
- 1 cup of coconut water, unsweetened,
- 1 orange, peeled,
- 2 cups of mango, frozen,
- 1 cup of pineapple, frozen,
- Juice of ½ a lime.

Instructions:
- Place all of the ingredients into a blender and blend until completely smooth.
- Serve immediately.

Pre-Workout Fiber Kick

Ingredients:
- 2 cups of fresh spinach,
- 2 cups of almond milk,
- 1 large green apple, cored,
- 1 banana,
- 1/3 cup of rolled oats,
- 1 tablespoon coconut oil,
- ½ teaspoon ground cinnamon.

Instructions:
- Place all of the ingredients into a blender and blend until completely smooth.
- Serve immediately.

Shamrock Smoothie

Ingredients:
- 2 cups of coconut milk, unsweetened,
- 1 ½ cups of fresh spinach,
- ½ cup of fresh mint leaves,
- 2 bananas,
- 4 medjool dates, pitted,
- 1 teaspoon of vanilla extract.

Instructions:
- Place all of the ingredients into a blender and blend until completely smooth.
- Serve immediately.

Jessica Brooks

Two To Mango

Ingredients:
- 2 cups of fresh spinach,
- 1 ½ cups of water,
- 2 cups of frozen mango,
- 1 orange, peeled,
- ¼ cup of rolled oats.

Instructions:
- Place all of the ingredients into a blender and blend until completely smooth.
- Serve immediately.

Green Tart

Ingredients:
- 2 cups of curly kale,
- 1 cup of water,
- 2 large stalks of celery,
- ½ a cucumber,
- 1/3 of a pink grapefruit,
- 1 cup of frozen pineapple.

Instructions:
- Place all of the ingredients into a blender and blend until completely smooth.
- Serve immediately.

Turmeric Booster

Ingredients:
- 2 cups of kale,
- 2 cups of coconut milk,
- 2 cups of pineapple,
- 1 cup of mango,
- Juice of ½ a lemon,
- 1 tablespoon of fresh ginger,
- ½ teaspoon of ground turmeric.

Instructions:
- Place all of the ingredients into a blender and blend until completely smooth.
- Serve immediately.

M-M

Ingredients:
- 2 cups of spinach,
- 2 cups of coconut water,
- 1 ½ cups of diced mango,
- 1 ½ cups of diced melon.

Instructions:
- Place all of the ingredients into a blender and blend until completely smooth.
- Serve immediately.

Cinnaberry Green

Ingredients:
- 2 cups of green chards,
- 2 cups of almond milk,
- 2 cups of mixed frozen berries,
- 1 banana,
- ½ teaspoon of ground cinnamon.

Instructions:
- Place all of the ingredients into a blender and blend until completely smooth.
- Serve immediately.

Top Twenty Refreshing Green Smoothies

The BCK Refreshener

Ingredients:

- 1 banana,
- 1 cup coconut milk,
- ½ cup fresh mint,
- Dash of cinnamon,
- 1 cup of ice,

Instructions:

It's probably best to blend the banana first and then add the coconut milk together with the rest of the ingredients. You can add ½ a cup of fresh pineapple in the mix as it's always a good combination with banana and coconut.

Açai Restart

Ingredients:

- 1 pack frozen açai puree (unsweetened),
- 1 banana,
- 1 cup pomegranate juice,
- 1 cup fresh raspberries,
- ½ cup baby spinach,
- 2 tablespoons aloe vera juice,
- 1 teaspoon macadamia nut oil,
- 2 teaspoons chia seed.

Instructions:

The frozen açai puree acts as the ice and main flavor in this exotic Amazonian recipe. Brazilian surfers promoted the açai berry as a supplement full of nutritional values and a smoothie based on it sounds very refreshing and tasty. Blend the açai pure with the fresh raspberries and add the pomegranate juice together with the aloe vera juice after a while. When you get a solid mixture just add the banana together with the chia seed and macadamia nut oil.

Watermelon and Coconut Rehydratation

Ingredients:

- 1 cup diced watermelon,
- ½ cup coconut water,
- ½ cup fresh mint,
- 2 tablespoons lime juice,
- 3 mint leaves,
- 5 ice cubes.

Instructions:

Watermelon combined with coconut water is the best natural source of electrolytes and that's why this smoothie is best served after an intensive physical activity. Just put everything together and turn on the blender. Very simple to make yet very tasteful.

Jessica Brooks

Keach on The Beach

Ingredients:

- 2 fresh peaches, diced
- ½ cup almond milk
- ½ cup kale
- 3 ice cubes

Instructions:
Another fresh smoothie that will give you all the fructose you need in one day. Dice the peach, it's always better to use fresh ones, and blend it with the kale and almond milk before adding the ice.

6AM Orange n' Green Wakeup

Ingredients:

- 1 cup orange juice, freshly squeezed,
- 1 teaspoon turmeric,
- 1 cup water,
- ½ cup baby spinach,
- 2 tablespoons lemon juice.

Instructions:

When cleansing your metabolism you may feel like you're doing too much at times, with measuring foods to the gram and making tea every 20 minutes or something like that. That's why it's important to start your day as quick as possible. Put all the ingredients in a shaker cup and mix them without the need for a blender. If you have some fancy shaker, then you can use ice instead of water.

The Green Lantern

Ingredients:

- 1 cup water,
- 2 teabags or 2 teaspoons of green tea,
- ½ fresh peach, diced,
- ½ medium sized cucumber,
- ¼ cup parsley,
- ½ cup ice.

Instructions:

If this is not detox, then I don't know what is. Boil the green tea in one cup of water and wait for it to cool down. Mix everything else, including the parsley, in the blender and add the cooled down green tea at the end. You will get a smoothie detox bomb that should keep you energized and full till dinner time.

LOCo Smoothie (Lemon-Orange-Citrus)

Ingredients

- 1 cup soy milk
- 1 orange, peeled and sliced
- ½ cup citrus juice
- ¼ cup lemon juice
- ½ cup ice cubes
- ½ cup fresh mint

Instructions:

Peel the orange and slice it on small chunks. Make sure that there are no seeds or white parts in the citrus juice because it will make the whole smoothie bitter. Mix everything in the blender and add a dash of cinnamon on the top.

Applime

Ingredients:

- ½ cup soy milk,
- ½ cup coconut milk,
- 1 cup fresh green apple, diced and peeled,
- 2 tablespoons lime juice,
- 1 small kiwi, peeled and diced,
- 1 cup ice cubes.

Instructions:

After you peel the kiwi and dice it together with the apple, mix all the ingredients and blend them for about half a minute to one minute. You'll get an interesting green mixture that will help you lose weight and cleanse your metabolism.

Pineapple Express

Ingredients:

- 1 cup fresh pineapple,
- 1 cup coconut milk,
- ½ medium sized fresh mango, diced,
- ½ cup fresh mint,
- 1 teaspoon macadamia nut oil,
- 1 cup ice cubes.

Instructions:

This is the one that you've been waiting for. It's probably the smoothie with the best taste on the list and it takes only one spin of the blender to make it. Just put everything in the blender and you get a top notch smoothie for the morning, afternoon or evening.

Slimberry Straw

Ingredients:

- 1 cup fresh strawberries,
- ½ cup raspberries,
- ½ cup celery, diced,
- ½ cup fresh mint,
- ½ cup ice,

Instructions:

Strawberries and raspberries are a combo that yells weight loss. Add little bit of celery just for additional antioxidants. You can use frozen strawberries or even raspberries, depending from the season. If you do this, go easy on the ice. Blend everything for about a minute. You can add dash of mint for better taste.

The Spinora!

Ingredients:
- 1 navel orange, peeled
- 1 banana
- 1 cup spinach
- ¼ cup coconut water
- 1 tablespoon hemp seeds
- Ice cubes

Instructions:
- Place all of the ingredients into a blender and blend until completely smooth.
- Serve immediately.

Green Vs Orange

Ingredients:
- 1 ½ cups water
- 4 handfuls of spinach
- 4 romaine leaves
- 2 navel oranges, peeled
- 2 ripe bananas
- A small knob of ginger
- ½ of a cucumber

Instructions:
- Place all of the ingredients into a blender and blend until completely smooth.
- Serve immediately.

Summer Awakening

Ingredients:
- 1 cup green tea, chilled
- 1 cup of cilantro
- 1 cup of organic baby kale
- 1 cup of cucumber
- 1 cup of pineapple
- Juice of 1 lemon
- 1 tablespoon of fresh ginger
- ½ an avocado, pitted and skinned

Instructions:
- Place all of the ingredients into a blender and blend until completely smooth.
- Serve immediately.

Minty Honey

Ingredients:
- ½ honeydew melon, chunks
- ½ cup of coconut milk
- 2 leaves of fresh mint
- 1 teaspoon of fresh lime juice
- 1 cup of ice
- A drizzle of honey

Instructions:
- Place all of the ingredients into a blender and blend until completely smooth.
- Serve immediately.

The Energetic Green Monster!

Ingredients:
- 1 cup of coconut water
- 1/3 cup of coconut milk
- 1 tablespoon of agave nectar
- Juice of half a lime
- 1 pear, peeled and cored
- 2 handfuls of kale
- 2 handfuls of spinach

Instructions:
- Place all of the ingredients into a blender and blend until completely smooth.
- Serve immediately.

Green Goddess

Ingredients:
- ½ a cucumber
- 1 stalk of celery
- 1 handful of kale
- 1 green apple, cored and peeled
- 1 pear, cored and peeled
- 1 teaspoon of lemon juice

Instructions:
- Place all of the ingredients into a blender and blend until completely smooth.
- Serve immediately.

Easy Being Green

Ingredients:
- 2 green apples, cored and sliced
- 1 cup of honeydew melon, peeled
- 1 cup of seedless green grapes
- 1 handful of spinach
- 1 handful of kale
- 1 kiwi, peeled
- ½ a cucumber

Instructions:
- Place all of the ingredients into a blender and blend until completely smooth.
- Serve immediately.

Garden Refresher

Ingredients:
- 1 carrot, trimmed
- 2 celery stalks
- 1 red bell pepper, cored and seeded
- 2 tomatoes
- 1 handful of watercress
- 1 cucumber

Instructions:
- Place all of the ingredients into a blender and blend until completely smooth.
- Serve immediately.

Green Up and Go

Ingredients:
- 5 celery stalks
- 1 handful of kale
- 1 handful of spinach
- 10 stalks of parsley lead
- 1 lemon, peeled and sectioned
- 1 cucumber

Instructions:
- Place all of the ingredients into a blender and blend until completely smooth.
- Serve immediately.

The Green Glow

Ingredients:
- 1 ½ cups of water
- 1 head of romance lettuce
- A handful of spinach
- 3 stalks of celery
- 1 green apple, cored
- 1 pear, cored
- 1 banana
- Juice of ½ a lemon

Instructions:
- Place all of the ingredients into a blender and blend until completely smooth.
- Serve immediately.

Top Twenty Quick Breakfast Green Smoothies

Breakfast of Champs

Ingredients:

- 1 cup almond milk,
- ¼ cup almonds,
- ½ small banana,
- ½ mango,
- ¼ cup pineapple
- 1 scoop protein powder, vanilla flavor,
- ½ cup ice,
- ½ cup asparagus.

Instructions:

You'll get everything you need with this smoothie. The amount of the ingredients above will probably produce 2 servings, but don't worry as you can't get enough from this in the morning, so drinking 2 servings at once is not that bad at all. Mix the banana, mango and pineapple together with the almonds and the almond milk before adding everything else.

Breakfast of Champs Veggie Version

Ingredients:

- 1 cup baked pumpkin,
- 1 teaspoon honey,
- ½ cup orange juice,
- 1 cup carrots,
- ¼ cup hazelnuts,
- ½ cup ice,
- 1 teaspoon macadamia nut oil,
- 1 scoop protein powder.

Instructions:

This is probably the most complicated recipe in the book because you need to bake the pumpkin, but you can also use canned pumpkin puree to make things easier. Before you put everything in the blender make sure that the carrots are peeled. You can put a dash of cinnamon on top for taste.

Grapes, Coconut & Spinach

Ingredients:
- 1 cup seedless green grapes
- 1 cup baby spinach
- ½ cup ice
- ¼ cup coconut milk

Instructions:
Make sure that you get the seedless grapes as the taste is very different with grape seeds inside the smoothie. You can put everything together at once.

Jessica Brooks

Kiwi is the New Green

Ingredients:
- 1 cup almond milk,
- 1 cup brussels sprouts,
- 1 kiwi, peeled and chopped,
- ½ cup chopped pineapple,
- ½ cup ice.

Instructions:
Make sure that you peeled the kiwi and pineapple good enough before you blend them together with the almond milk and brussels sprouts. After you get a homogeneous mixture just add the ice and blend it for additional two minutes.

Groovy Smoothie

Ingredients:
- 1 banana, cut in chunks,
- 1 cup grapes,
- 6 ounces (1 tub) vanilla yogurt,
- ½ green apple,
- 1 ½ cups fresh spinach,
- ½ cup ice.

Instructions:
Again. Use seedless grapes for this one as well. The vanilla yogurt will make all the difference so you will want to add it at the beginning together with the ice and then start adding all the other ingredients.

Kaleastic

Ingredients:
- ½ cup coconut milk,
- 2 cups kale,
- 1 ½ cups pineapple,
- 1 medium sized banana,
- ½ cup raisins,
- 1 cup ice.

Instructions:
Before you start making this smoothie you need to steam the kale for around 1 minute. After you finish this add the kale together with everything else in the blender and blend until you get a smooth mixture and no ice chunks.

CinnApple

Ingredients:
- 1 cup apple juice,
- 1 pear,
- 1 green apple,
- 1 cup fresh spinach,
- 1 teaspoon cinnamon,
- ½ cup ice.

Instructions:
Core and slice the pear and apple before mixing them together with the apple juice and spinach. You can add the ice and cinnamon at the end and blend for two more minutes.

Zucchini, Chocolate & Banana Freeze

Ingredients:
- 1 cup zucchini, frozen,
- 2 medium bananas, frozen,
- 2 tablespoons cocoa powder,
- ¼ cup chopped peanuts,
- 1 cup ice.

Instructions:
Be careful not to get a brain freeze with this smoothie. After you blend all the ingredients you can rinse a little bit of dark chocolate on the top for taste.

Honeydew & Mint

Ingredients:
- 1 cucumber,
- 2 cups cubed honeydew melon,
- ½ cup lemon juice,
- ½ cup orange juice,
- ½ cup fresh mint,
- 2 cups crushed ice.

Instructions:
Peel, seed and chop the cucumber to get a better taste of your smoothie. If you want to get a stronger taste from the honeydew melon, then you should cut down on the lemon and orange juice. Replace them with soy milk instead.

Broccoli & Green Grapes

Ingredients:
- 2 cups broccoli,
- 1 cup green grapes,
- 1 cucumber,
- ½ cup water,
- ½ cup lime juice,
- ½ cup ice.

Instructions:
It doesn't go greener than this. Just make sure that you get seedless green grapes because, as we previously mentioned, the seeds can change the taste of your smoothie. After you make sure that you got the seedless type of grapes, chop the broccoli and peel the cucumber before putting everything in the blender.

Green Morning Fuel

Ingredients:
- 1 cup of oat milk,
- 1 cup of coconut water,
- 1 teaspoon of spirulina,
- 2 teaspoons of flaxseed,
- 1 tablespoon of organic coconut oil,
- ¼ cup frozen berries,
- 1 teaspoon probiotics,
- 2 tablespoons of natural yogurt,
- A pinch of cinnamon,
- 2 drops of stevia.

Instructions:
- Place all of the ingredients into a blender and blend until completely smooth.
- Serve immediately.

Green Vs Red

Ingredients:
Red layer:
- 1 frozen banana,
- 1 cup of strawberries,
- ½ cup of coconut water.

Green layer:
- 1 cup of spinach,
- ½ a frozen banana,
- ¼ cup pomegranate arils,
- ¼ cup of coconut water.

Instructions:
- Blend the ingredients for the green layer in your blender until smooth.
- Pour into the bottom half of your glass.
- Clean the blender and the blend the red layer until smooth.
- Pour on top of the green layer, for a cool, multilayered smoothie!

Mango & Coconut Green Smoothie

Ingredients:
- 1 cup of fresh spinach leaves,
- 1 cup of fresh mango cubes,
- ½ a banana,
- 1 cup of coconut milk,
- ½ cup of freshly squeezed orange juice,
- ½ cup of ice cubes.

Instructions:
- Place all of the ingredients into a blender and blend until completely smooth.
- Serve immediately.

Irish Green

Ingredients:

- ½ an avocado, pitted and skinned,
- ¼ cup of coconut milk,
- ¼ cup of fresh baby spinach,
- ¼ cup of fresh mint,
- 1 scoop of vanilla flavored protein powder,
- 2 tablespoons of pistachio nuts,
- 1 vanilla bean,
- 4 drops of stevia extract,
- ½ cup of water,
- Ice cubes.

Instructions:

- Place all of the ingredients into a blender and blend until completely smooth.
- Serve immediately.

BAMango

Ingredients:
- 2 bananas,
- 2 cups of kale or spinach,
- 1 mango, peeled,
- 3 tablespoons of hemp seeds,
- A handful of sprouts,
- ½ cup of unsweetened almond milk,
- Ice cubes.

Instructions:
- Place all of the ingredients into a blender and blend until completely smooth.
- Serve immediately.

Green Sunrise

Ingredients:
- 1 cup of spinach,
- 1 frozen banana,
- ½ of an avocado, pitted,
- ¼ cup of unsweetened almond milk,
- ½ teaspoon vanilla,
- ¼ teaspoon cinnamon.

Instructions:
- Place all of the ingredients into a blender and blend until completely smooth.
- Serve immediately.

Peanut Butter & Green Jelly Smoothie

Ingredients:
- Half a cup of vanilla Greek yogurt,
- 1 cup of mixed frozen berries,
- 1 tablespoon of peanut butter,
- ¾ cup of unsweetened almond milk,
- Handful of leafy greens,
- Ice cubes.

Instructions:
- Place all of the ingredients into a blender and blend until completely smooth.
- Serve immediately.

Green Lemon Cooler

Ingredients:
- ½ a lemon peeled and deseeded,
- 5 large basil leaves,
- ¼ a cucumber,
- 2 frozen bananas,
- 2 inches of fresh aloe gel,
- 1 cup of water.

Instructions:
- Place all of the ingredients into a blender and blend until completely smooth.
- Serve immediately.

Red Grape and Fig Smoothie

Ingredients:
- 5 medium figs,
- 1 cup of red grapes,
- ½ head of romaine lettuce,
- 2 organic bananas,
- 1 cup of water.

Instructions:
- Place all of the ingredients into a blender and blend until completely smooth.
- Serve immediately.

Beety Greens

Ingredients:
- 2 small bananas,
- 1 cup of red grapes,
- 2 teaspoons of chia seeds,
- 1 cup of beet greens,
- 1 cup of water.

Instructions:
- Place all of the ingredients into a blender and blend until completely smooth.
- Serve immediately.

Top Twenty Cleansing/Detox Green Smoothies

Ginger Man

Ingredients
- ½ cup vanilla Greek yogurt,
- 1 pear,
- 1 cup pear juice/coconut water,
- ¼ cup fresh ginger root/1 teaspoon dried ground ginger,
- 2 cups baby spinach,
- 1 tablespoon flaxseed,
- ½ cup ice.

Instructions:
Boil the ginger until soft and then peel. Wait before the ginger is cold enough and mix it together with the Greek yogurt. Core the pear and add it to the mixture together with the pear juice or coconut water by your choice. When you get a smooth mixture just add the rest of the ingredients and blend for an additional minute.

Metabolism Booster

Ingredients:
- 1 cup almond milk,
- ¼ cup almonds,
- ¼ cup broccoli,
- 1 cup strawberries,
- ¼ cup cannellini,
- 2 teaspoons green tea,
- 1 teaspoon flaxseed,
- ½ teaspoon cinnamon,
- ½ cup ice.

Instructions:
Get rid of the broccoli stems and prepare it on steam for couple of minutes, just to get soft. After it has cooled down add it together with the strawberries, almonds and almond milk and blend for about a minute before you add the cannellini, flaxseed and cinnamon. Boil the green tea in ½ cup of water and add it together with the ice at the end.

Recovery Helper

Ingredients:
- 1 cup frozen cherries,
- 1 cup strawberries,
- 1 cup kale,
- ¼ cup walnuts,
- 1 teaspoon wheat germ,
- ½ teaspoon freshly grated ginger,
- 1 teaspoon green tea,
- ½ cup ice.

Instructions:
You can use green tea in teabags as well. Boil the green tea and wait for it to cool down. After that just put it in the blender with everything else and blend for about two minutes or until you get a smooth mixture.

Spinach Mojito

Ingredients:

- ½ cup coconut water,
- 1 banana,
- 1 cup spinach,
- ½ small lime,
- 1 teaspoon green tea,
- ½ cup fresh mint,
- 1 cup ice.

Instructions:

Boil the green tea in ½ cup of water and let it cool down. Juice the lime and add the juice together with the coconut water, banana and spinach. Blend for about a minute before adding the green tea, fresh mint and ice. Continue for two more minutes.

Mango-Kiwi Fat Burner

Ingredients:
- 1 cup non-fat vanilla kefir,
- 1 cup spinach,
- ½ cup frozen blueberries,
- ½ cup mango,
- 1 kiwi,
- ¼ cup parsley,
- ¼ cup cashews,
- 1 teaspoon flaxseed,
- ¼ cup celery sticks,
- ¾ cup ice.

Instructions:
Make sure that you peel the kiwi before you put it together with the vanilla kefir, spinach, blueberries and mango in the blender. After a minute or so add the parsley, cashews flaxseed and celery. When you get a fine mixture add the ice and blend until you get a smooth mixture.

Avocado Aloe Cleanser

Ingredients:
- 1 cup spinach,
- 1 banana,
- ¼ cup avocado,
- 1 cup coconut water,
- 1 tablespoon aloe vera juice,
- 1 lemon,
- Dash of cayenne pepper,
- ½ cup ice.

Instructions:
Juice the lemon and add the juice together with the spinach, banana and avocado. Put the ice together with the aloe vera juice, coconut water and add a dash of cayenne pepper on top for taste.

Sweet Spinach Antioxidant

Ingredients:
- 2 cups spinach,
- 1 pear,
- ½ cup red grapes,
- ½ cup fat-free kefir,
- ⅓ cup avocado,
- ¼ cup lime juice,
- 1 cup ice.

Instructions:
Core the pear and put it in the blender together with the red grapes, spinach and kefir. Make sure that you get grapes with seeds because they're a great antioxidant. Add the ice, avocado and lime juice at the end.

PBS Antioxidant (Pumpkin, Banana & Spinach)

Ingredients:
- ½ cup organic pumpkin puree,
- 1 large banana,
- 1 cup spinach,
- 1/2 cup almond milk,
- 1 dash cinnamon,
- 10 prunes,
- 1 cup ice.

Instructions:
You can use a baked pumpkin, but this will take you more time. Leave the cinnamon and prunes for the end together with the ice as you want to get maximum flavor from them.

Ginger Orange Detox

Ingredients:

- 1 cup spinach,
- ½ cup romaine lettuce,
- 2 oranges,
- 1 banana,
- ½ cup carrots,
- ¼ cup ginger root,
- ½ cup cucumber,
- ½ cup ice.

Instructions:

Boil the ginger root until it gets soft and peel it. Put it together with the oranges and spinach before adding the carrots, romaine lettuce, ice and cucumber. Blend for around 2 minutes.

Jessica Brooks

Blueberry Mint Delight

Ingredients:
2 cups spinach,
2 cups blueberry,
1 kiwi,
¼ cup fresh mint,
1 cup coconut water,
1 cup ice.

Instructions:
It's good to use frozen blueberries for better taste, but you can use fresh ones as well. Blend them together with the peeled kiwi and spinach before adding the mint, coconut water and ice.

Cranberry Cleanser

Ingredients:
- 2 cups of kale,
- 1 cup of water,
- 1 cup of cranberries,
- 2 oranges, peeled,
- 2 bananas.

Instructions:
- Place all of the ingredients into a blender and blend until completely smooth.
- Serve immediately.

Ginger Spice Smoothie

Ingredients:
- 1 nub of ginger root,
- 1 teaspoon of ground cinnamon,
- 2 cups of spinach,
- 1 cup of water.

Instructions:
- Place all of the ingredients into a blender and blend until completely smooth.
- Serve immediately.

Green and Clean Smoothie

Ingredients:
- ¼ of a cucumber,
- 1 cup of spinach,
- ½ an avocado, pitted,
- 1 celery stalk,
- 2 sprigs of fresh mint,
- 1 kiwi fruit, peeled,
- 1 cup of water,
- ½ a green apple, cored,
- A squirt of lemon juice.

Instructions:
- Place all of the ingredients into a blender and blend until completely smooth.
- Serve immediately.

Extreme Detox Smoothie

Ingredients:
- ½ a carrot, peeled,
- ½ a pear, cored,
- ½ cup of broccoli florets,
- 1 cup of water.

Instructions:
- Place all of the ingredients into a blender and blend until completely smooth.
- Serve immediately.

Super Green, Super Clean

Ingredients:
- 1 ¼ cups of kale,
- 1 ¼ cups of frozen mango,
- 2 ribs of celery,
- 1 cup of fresh tangerine juice,
- ¼ cup of flat-leaf parsley,
- ¼ cup of fresh mint.

Instructions:
- Place all of the ingredients into a blender and blend until completely smooth.
- Serve immediately.

Hale to the Kale

Ingredients:
- ½ a pear, cored,
- ¼ of an avocado, pitted,
- ½ of a cucumber,
- ½ of a lemon,
- Handful of cilantro,
- 1 cup of kale,
- A small chunk of ginger,
- ½ cup of coconut water,
- 1 scoop of pea protein powder,
- 1 cup of water.

Instructions:
- Place all of the ingredients into a blender and blend until completely smooth.
- Serve immediately.

Sweet Spirulina

Ingredients:
- ½ a banana,
- ½ cup of blueberries, frozen,
- ¼ of an avocado, pitted,
- ¼ of a cucumber,
- ½ cup of almond milk,
- 1 teaspoon of spirulina,
- 1 scoop of vanilla, pea protein powder,
- 1 cup of water.

Instructions:
- Place all of the ingredients into a blender and blend until completely smooth.
- Serve immediately.

The Bliss of Alkalinity

Ingredients:
- ½ of a pear, cored,
- ¼ of an avocado,
- 1 cup of spinach,
- ¼ cup of coconut water,
- 1 teaspoon of chia seeds.

Instructions:
- Place all of the ingredients into a blender and blend until completely smooth.
- Serve immediately.

Jicama

Ingredients:
- 5 large romaine lettuce leaves,
- ½ of a granny smith apple, cored,
- ¼ of an avocado,
- ½ a cucumber,
- ½ cup of jicama,
- A handful of cilantro,
- 1 whole lime,
- 1 medjool date,
- 1 cup of water.

Instructions:
- Place all of the ingredients into a blender and blend until completely smooth.
- Serve immediately.

Tangy Green Detox

Ingredients:
- 1 large cucumber,
- A handful of kale,
- A handful of romaine,
- 2 stalks of celery,
- 1 big broccoli stem,
- 1 green apple, cored,
- ½ peeled lemon, seeded.

Instructions:
- Place all of the ingredients into a blender and blend until completely smooth.
- Serve immediately.

Top Ten Pure Green Smoothies

Refreshingly Green

Ingredients:
- ½ a cucumber,
- ½ cup of fresh basil,
- 1 cup of spring mix,
- 1 tablespoon of coconut oil,
- 2 cups of fresh green beans,
- 5 chives,
- ½ cup of water.

Instructions:
- Place all of the ingredients into a blender and blend until completely smooth.
- Serve immediately.

Sweet Nothings

Ingredients:
- 2 cups of water,
- ½ a head of romaine lettuce,
- 1 cucumber,
- 2 stalks of celery,
- 3 cups of spinach,
- Ice cubes
- 1 handful of fresh parsley.

Instructions:
- Place all of the ingredients into a blender and blend until completely smooth.
- Serve immediately.

Simplicity

Ingredients:
- 2 cups of spinach,
- 2 green apples, cored and chopped,
- A dash of lime juice.

Instructions:
- Place all of the ingredients into a blender and blend until completely smooth.
- Serve immediately.

Kiwi Gladness

Ingredients:
- 3 kiwis, peeled,
- 3 cups of spinach,
- 1 cup of water.

Instructions:
- Place all of the ingredients into a blender and blend until completely smooth.
- Serve immediately.

Green For Life

Ingredients:
- 2 granny smith apples, cored,
- ½ of an avocado, pitted,
- 3 kiwis, skinned,
- 2 cups of spinach,
- 1 cup of water.

Instructions:
- Place all of the ingredients into a blender and blend until completely smooth.
- Serve immediately.

Lean and Green

Ingredients:
- 3 cups of ice cubes,
- 1 cup of green grapes,
- 1 cucumber,
- ½ cup of broccoli florets,
- 1 sprig of fresh mint.

Instructions:
- Place all of the ingredients into a blender and blend until completely smooth.
- Serve immediately.

Zucchini

Ingredients:
- 1 zucchini, cubed,
- 5 ice cubes,
- 1 cup of apple juice,
- 2 tablespoons of sweetener,
- Splash of lime juice.

Instructions:
- Place all of the ingredients into a blender and blend until completely smooth.
- Serve immediately.

Endless Green Energy

Ingredients:
- 1 cup of almond milk,
- 1 cup of fresh spinach,
- 1 kiwi, peeled,
- ½ of a cucumber,
- ½ cup of ice.

Instructions:
- Place all of the ingredients into a blender and blend until completely smooth.
- Serve immediately.

Can You Stomach It?

Ingredients:
- 1 teaspoons of wheat grass,
- 1 teaspoon of spirulina,
- 1 teaspoon of chlorella,
- 1 teaspoon of barley grass.

Instructions:
- Mix the ingredients in a glass.
- Hold your nose for this one!
- The health benefits of this drink are simple staggering.

Cool Kale Smoothie

Ingredients:
- 2 cups of green grapes,
- 2 cups of kale,
- 1 cup of ice cubes.

Instructions:
- Place all of the ingredients into a blender and blend until completely smooth.
- Serve immediately.

Free Ebook Offer
The Ultimate Guide To Vitamins

I'm very excited to be able to make this offer to you. This is a wonderful 10k word ebook that has been made available to you through my publisher, Valerian Press. As a health conscious person you should be well aware of the uses and health benefits of each of the vitamins that should make up our diet. This book gives you an easy to understand, scientific explanation of the vitamin followed by the recommended daily dosage. It then highlights all the important health benefits of each vitamin. A list of the best sources of each vitamin is provided and you are also given some actionable next steps for each vitamin to make sure you are utilizing the information!

As well as receiving the free ebooks you will also be sent a weekly stream of free ebooks, again from my publishing company Valerian Press. You can expect to receive at least a new, free ebook each and every week. Sometimes you might receive a massive 10 free books in a week!

All you need to do is simply type this link into your browser: http://bit.ly/18hmup4

About the Author

Hello! I'm Jessica Brooks, relatively new to the world of authorship but a veteran of the health and diet industry. If you have read any of my books, I would like to thank you from the bottom of my heart. I truly hope they have helped answer your questions and injected some inspiration into your life. Thanks to my wonderful upbringing I have been a vegetarian since infancy, making to jump to veganism nearly 20 years ago. I'm passionate about helping people improve their health! Over the coming months I am hoping to write a couple more books that will help people learn, start and succeed with certain diets.

In my spare time I am an avid reader of fantasy fiction (George Martin, you demon!). You can often find me lounging in my hammock with my latest book well into the evening. Outside of reading, I love all things physical. From hiking to sailing, swimming to skiing I'm a fan of it all! I try to practice Yoga a couple of times a week, I really recommend everyone gives it a try. You will just feel amazing after a good session!

You can find a facebook page I help manage here:

https://www.facebook.com/CleanFoodDiet

I would like to thank my publishers Valerian Press for giving me the opportunity to create this book.

Valerian Press

At Valerian Press we have three key beliefs.

Providing outstanding value: We believe in enriching all of our customers' lives, doing everything we can to ensure the best experience.

Championing new talent: We believe in showcasing the worlds emerging talent by giving them the platform to grow.

Simplicity and efficiency: We understand how valuable your time is. Our products are stream-lined and consist only of what you want. You will find no fluff with us.

We hope you have enjoyed reading Jessica's Smoothie Recipe book.

We would love to offer you a regular supply of our free and discounted books. We cover a huge range of non-fiction genres; diet and cookbooks, health and fitness, alternative and holistic medicine, spirituality and plenty more. All you need to do is simply type this link into your web browser:
http://bit.ly/18hmup4

Free Preview of "Vegan Slow Cooker Cookbook: 100 Delicious Recipes"

Tempeh chili with Vaquero beans

It's a protein packed dish for a healthy meal. Serve it over rice or quinoa for a hearty lunch or dinner.

Serves: 6

Ingredients:

- Olive oil – 2 tablespoons
- Onion – ½ small, minced
- Garlic – 3 cloves, minced
- Soy tempeh – 8 ounces, diced
- Cooked Vaquero beans – 6 cups or Pinto beans – 3 cans, rinsed and drained
- Water – 4 cups
- Tomatoes – 1 can, diced
- Tomato paste – 1 tablespoon
- Chili powder – 1 teaspoon
- Pasilla chile powder – 1 teaspoon
- Oregano – 1 teaspoon
- Paprika – 1 /2 teaspoon
- Chipotle powder – ¼-1/2 teaspoon
- Plain or smoked salt, to taste
- Cashew cream or vegan sour cream, for serving

Method

In a pan, heat olive oil and sauté onion until tender and translucent. Then add garlic and again stir fry for a few minutes. Remove from the pan. With all the other ingredients except sour cream, put onion-garlic in a slow cooker. Turn on the cooker on high and cook for 4-5 hours.

While serving, top it up with a little sour cream and enjoy!

Vegan Slow cooker Cincinnati Chili

It's a great spaghetti topping for a wholesome meal. Enjoy it either in lunch or at dinner or amuse your guests with its amazing flavors!

Note: Prepare the chili a day before if you want to devour it for lunch.

Serves: 2

Ingredients:
For morning
- Dry black beluga lentils – ¾ cup (use any other lentil if you do not want dark color chili)
- Water – 1 ½ cups
- Garlic – 2 cloves, minced
- Bay leaf – 1
- Grounded vegan crumbles – ½ cup (if you want a soy free version, then use cooked quinoa – ½ cup)
- Ground cumin – 1/2 teaspoon
- Ground hot pepper (any) – ¼ teaspoon
- Ground cinnamon – 1/8 teaspoon
- Chili powder – 1 teaspoon
- Cocoa powder – 1 teaspoon
- Ground allspice – 1 pinch

For evening
- Tomatoes – 1 ½ cups, diced
- Fresh ground nutmeg – a dash
- Salt, to taste
- Cooked pasta – 2-3 cups (for serving)

Method
In the morning, add all the morning ingredients in a 1 ½- 2 quart slow cooker and cook on low for 7-9 hours.

Half an hour before serving, open the cooker and add tomatoes, salt and nutmeg. Cook on high until the tomatoes get smashed and mixed with other ingredients.

Serve hot over cooked pasta and top it up with chopped onions or shredded vegan cheese or cooked beans, all optional though.

Grains and beans slow cooker chili

Chili can never go wrong as a main dish. It works well if you are in a mood to have a family get together or are planning for a formal event. Top it over cooked rice or pasta or simply eat with a taco or quesadillas, you'll love it all the time!

Serves: 3-4

Ingredients:
- Assorted dry beans (no kidney beans) – 2 cups
- Water – 6 cups
- Tomato puree or diced tomatoes – 1 can
- Millet – 1/8 cup
- Dry vegan bouillon – 1 tablespoon
- Cumin – 1 teaspoon
- Chili spice mix – 1 teaspoon
- Ancho powder or chipotle – ½ teaspoon
- Smoked paprika – ½ teaspoon
- Salt, to taste

Method
In a 1-1 ½ quart slow cooker, add beans and 4 cups water at night. Cook for 7-9 hours or overnight on low temperature.

In the morning, remove the beans from the cooker and rinse them. Again add beans with all other ingredients and 2 cups water. Add salt before serving. Now let everything cook on low for 7-10 hours.

Crockpot vegan bean chili with steel-cut oats

Chili is for all seasons and this one is a perfect main dish to be served over cooked quinoa or rice.

Serves: 6

Ingredients:
- Water – 6 cups
- Veggie bouillon – 2 cubes
- Steel-cut oats – 1 /2 cup
- Oregano – 1 tablespoon
- Ground cumin – 2 teaspoons
- Chili powder – 1 teaspoon
- Garlic – 3 cloves, minced
- Kidney beans – 1-14.5 ounces can, drained and rinsed
- Black beans - 1-14.5 ounces can, drained and rinsed
- Tomatoes - 1-14.5 ounces can, diced
- Fire-roasted or regular frozen corns – 1 cup
- Liquid smoke, to taste
- ½ lime juice
- Salt and pepper, to taste

Method
In a 1-1 ½ quart slow cooker, add everything except lime juice and salt & pepper.

Cook for 7-10 hours on low heat. Before serving, add salt & pepper and squeeze ½ lime over chili.

To grab this exciting vegan/vegetarian cookbook be sure to search for Jessica Brooks in the Kindle Store or on Amazon's book store!

Jessica Brooks

15320849R00071

Printed in Poland
by Amazon Fulfillment
Poland Sp. z o.o., Wrocław